C000120754

For more information visit our website: https://www.chifull.eu/

For contact mail us at chifull.eu@outlook.com

Introduction

In this book, we introduce you to some essential concepts from the old teachings of the Dao.

We have chosen this curriculum structure because of the applicability and accuracy in our current time.

The goal is to encourage you to look at this world in a different and refreshing way. In addition, these insights can help you to give a different turn to your life by yourself, maybe also to take a step back (or a number of steps) and see where you really are.

We would like to recommend you to create a personal journal for yourself in which you can write your own findings and answers/insights, it is your inner journey and the book can still sometimes serve as a reference book. It can also happen that suddenly answers emerge from within, completely automatically and from your own being.

We have kept the content as concise as possible, on our website we want to offer more online modules by subject. These can be added to this book so that a complete course is created. At the end of this book, you will find more information about our method.

We wish you Good Chi!

Chi-Full team

A short history of the Daoist key books

The earliest Daoism arose at the time of the Yellow Emperor and can be found in 'The Yellow Emperor's Inner Canon'. It contains an extensive treatise on the health of the human body related to the seasons and other cosmic laws. It is a book that is difficult to access to the layman, although there are plenty of things worth knowing to be found between the lines (for those who want to take on the challenge).

The first book is the I Ching (Book of Changes), this is one of the most detailed guides of human development. It translates all developments through phases, that we will not elaborate further in this basic book.

The second book is the Dao De Jing (Lao-Tse), which is written in a time of social decline and disorder. It was a period of decay of an old social order, and the scriptures were mainly on socio-political matters, reviewed against the light of the Dao. That is why you find a lot of advice to leaders in the Dao De Jing. Many comments and distinctive literature are based on the Dao De Jing. *)

The third book is the Chuang-Tzu, it was written during a period of political decay, characterized by growing militarism and a dominant force on social contracts. The sphere in the book is more that of humorous withdrawal, anarchy, satire, and unrestrained imagination. It is called the first fantasy work in China's history, a dramatic discharge of spirit, and one of the greatest masterpieces of all time.

Daoïsm is not sentimental and has always recognized the reality of the presence of war, but is at its core pacifistic. With regard to war, there is a realistic approach. There is a preventive approach, that focuses on minimizing the reasons for war that is latent present in the human psyche (consciousness). There is a palliative approach, that focuses on minimizing war trauma as soon as something like this really takes place.

The above-mentioned matters were issues in the earliest Daoïst history and are the basis of the Daoïst views. This covers up the period to the third century before Christ.

After that a Daoïstic laissez-faire management arose within the then created Han dynasty, that announced a period of economic recovery. From that moment on there was a growing interest in natural sciences, especially agriculture and technology. But also an extensive exchange between Daoism and Confucianism emerged, in which various Daoïst views were included within the Confucian doctrine. We could conclude from this that the original Daoïsm has become distorted from that moment on, the views presented by Lao-Tse in the Dao De Jing have been edited by 'others' in various ways.

We work from the old original writings of both the Yellow Emperor and his 'Inner Canon', the I Ching, the Dao De Jing, and the Chuang-Tzu. But also the Hua-Hu-Ching, which turns out to be writing exported to the West at the time of tensions in China and is an extension to the Dao De Jing.

These books are at the basis of Daoïsm as it is practiced today in most Daoïst temples in China.

On the other hand, we are aware that all forms of -ism(e) appear to the reader, student and practitioner as forms of institute, rules and/or religion. If we were to convert an -ism(e) to English, then we would get 'is me' and then we would get stuck, especially when it comes to consciousness. We are nothing of that when we are concerned with all-encompassing infinite Awareness, which we essentially truly are, and want to expand and shift our boundaries in it.

We feel, the aforementioned books are aimed at making the readers more aware of their inner life, they want to challenge them and offer recurring ideas every day about which can be thought about or where the intuition can get free rein to sense what is meant. The books also deal with the pre-natal, intangible, unnamable, as well as life in this universe and the cyclic movements of the cosmos as we can perceive them ourselves.

It is up to the reader's understanding, his receptiveness to the texts in the books, to grow individually and to gain a broader understanding.

Which is most important, is that the books have no origin in the form of worship of gods or persons above the individual. The books work from an open space, from receptivity and awareness, from a resonance that may or may not be picked up by the reader.

They do not impose rules, no norms, no authority, but appeal only to the healthy feeling and understanding of the practitioner on his inner individual path in this life.

That is why we present these books with pleasure to our students and interested parties, it is a kind of foundation in this sometimes chaotic world and can serve as a foothold to experience a great time as a human being. Although they are really old, the content is certainly still applicable to our current time frame.

Absolute Truth

Although the Daoïst teaching comes pretty close to the truth, it is actually so that the Absolute Truth is nowhere member of.

The Absolute Truth is pure Awareness (1) and translates, from a different layer of understanding, into Consciousness (2). The latter is the area where Yin and Yang work together and make all energetically perceptible changes take place. These changes can also be perceived consciously by you so that you/the observer will start seeing the world in a different way.

This is not yet easily perceptible for the fully material-oriented people. They see what they see as real and cannot yet bridge the energetic tissue that lies under this manifestation (that which you see). On the other hand, it also has to do with where the focus and attention go, or where the individual interest lies and with what the person identifies himself.

Energy follows attention

With that, we could say: 'Energy follows attention'. And then you can test whether this is really happening within this manifestation by concentrating your attention enormously (hyperfocus) and then seeing what appears before you.

You have to know for sure what you want, because before you know it you may end up in something that you will not be happy about if you reflect on it. And you cannot know if or when the requested will arrive, it may come at a timing when you do not want it anymore.

But if this position is correct, then every individual could be able to 'conjure' that which he desires if he prays or begs hard enough.

With that, it is important to realize that negative energy - negative attention - also gets an effect. Even if it is only the negative attention that you give (and that you are leaking energy with that) to all sorts of things happening in this world.

Know that the so-called major players in this world receive al lot of energy through other people and that therefore you may unwantedly sponsor certain people with your energy, for things that you would wish to cease to exist.

We would like to point out that the greatest interest for you is, that from now on you only focus your energy on your own body-mind and spirit and that you are going to take care for your own wellbeing. Only when you are entirely in order, in balance and harmony, you will be brighter present in this world. You will start to see more clearly what is helping you and what does not, what is pure and what is toxic.

We also want to emphasize that what we say here is independent of spirituality as it is being propagated in the world right now. Which is in fact aimed at a feel-good content that lets you get into a fantasy world, where you are kept nice and cozy and are being led floating from one 'fairytale' to another 'fairytale'. It is a different kind of travel agency, where you get the feeling that you have experienced a lot, but if you really take a look inside yourself you will encounter the same unhappy person (Ego-mind) as before you started that journey.

Within the spiritual circuit, there is also offered a variety of courses, with an equally wide range of sometimes complex practices. There is also a quite huge (sometimes very expensive) price tag on it, it has gone miles away from the plainness and simplicity of the original teachings of the Dao. The route back to your natural inner self is simpler than simple, there are no complicated materials needed nor complicated grueling workouts or exercises.

It requires from you only to be totally present, to dare to open yourself to life itself and to the experiences that life has in store for you personally. As such, that you dare to start living from the sense that you are a unique appearance in this world. That it is not necessary for it to pick all sorts of bells and whistles from the stable to mold a personality, but that you are already carrying a natural inner state of being - an inner source of wisdom - that is founded in 'on-being-so-as-itself'. You can let yourself fall back into it, to see for yourself that you will keep much more energy for yourself because you do not worry anymore about the experiences life is throwing on your way. You then come back into acceptance, feel that everything is fine as it is and the need to change everything disappears. You actually stop to resist the flow of life itself.

You might even need to know how much energy it takes to maintain or rig your daily role, or change it to an even flashier of better performing/popular 'little model' for the outside world. And we do not only speak about life energy but also about time and money.

And yes, you will save a lot of time and money as your consciousness changes and you are able to accept yourself completely. The time you saved can be used to enjoy what the universe - life - has to offer you, exactly where you are now.

We want to show you who you truly are, to let you experience yourself again and actually to make sure that the mirror you are looking in right now gets cleared from dust. How nice would it be, to finally look in a clear mirror and be completely satisfied with yourself? In other words, we could say that every organism has its own perception which finds its origin in absolute Awareness, but seems to go a 'life' within Consciousness and there it individually experiences from the mind (through the senses). It is the perception of the individual showing at what level of understanding (Consciousness) it is. And speaking from that point of view it seems that there is an infinite 'layering'.

Really all you perceive around you comes from the One and is temporarily experienced as a form until its useful life is over. We could also say that the invisible is able to make itself visible through densification of energy. It is a contraction of small particles in a mold.

It is the person who thinks he is the body and no more than that, but the body is a universe in itself (with all things like cells, blood, organs, etc. in there). All the aforementioned parts of the body themselves are also Consciousness either Awareness.

As far as we can experience through our body, bacteria, viruses, and cells lead their own lives and carry their own form of Consciousness. In addition, there is a variety of forms of Consciousness in the cosmos that influence the human body, seen and unseen.

Consciousness is the domain in which the human mind is housed, Awareness is not in the same mansion and will not be touched by anything. Awareness is untouchable and thus seems to be a kind of protection (reservoir) against all the calamity that takes place on earth. There is absolutely nothing that can threaten, destroy corrupt Awareness. Awareness is not mutable and only seems to be a donor supplying and delivering 'energy'.

About Awareness, there is nothing to say, except that it Is.

Consciousness is, therefore, the domain where all activities can take place and where a dynamic (motion) is detected which occurs as experience.

If we now take a mandala of colored sand as an example, as it is made in temples with much attention and concentration. The most beautiful creations are made, but in the end, all of the colored sand is swept in a heap as the mandala is erased. There is nothing (other than a small residue of mixed and colored sand).

If we look at this principle in the temporary existence of us people, there could probably remain a residue of energy, invisible and intangible, returned to its original pre-natal form but still a kind of information medium at an energetical level.

Coming back to the Dao and the teachings of Daoism, we could explain the Dao as Awareness (1) as well as Consciousness (2).

Apparently, Awareness knows how to project Itself as Consciousness and all forms that rise-shine-dawn in it. Therefore, everything that is Consciousness is at the same time also Awareness. But by far not all forms are showing that they are being aware (able to understand) that their original state is Unchanging Awareness.

Before everything manifests itself, first there is a pattern of energy that connects everything with each other. It is an invisible tissue, or web, where everything is interconnected (actually the World Wide Web is almost a visible variant, whereby the diversity at once becomes apparent in all its complexity).

It is possible to have glimpses of Awareness when looking from Consciousness, where we have the ability to bring us as far as possible in alignment with Awareness. This means that we get into an increasingly vague area that we can not elaborate on as the refinement of perception increases. It gradually becomes more subtle.

Nature

Daoism actually is teaching fully connected to the natural forces, in which the person continuously connects with the cosmic forces that surround him and also constantly focuses on that.

These are observable in all kinds of ways in nature, the seasons, the weather, the rhythms of the human body, but also all organic forms that are visible and invisible and give off their own energy.

This form of observation can only take place, and develop more and more deeply if man is able to come to a standstill and rest. For the Daoïst a life of serenity, peacefulness, rest and silence is the highest good. That does not mean he is a lazybones. He surfs as it were, on the waves of the cosmos, the natural energies manifesting themselves. He lets the artificial world pass by and sees it for what it is.

If he does not, his perception may become disturbed and at the same time the serene tranquility and clarity with that. The Daoïst appreciates the simplicity of natural living and is satisfied with the simple things he does. He does not interfere with the creations of others, he surely is able to be with others, but then each time turns back to himself (his true inner serenity and peace). He thus maintains his own energy field and over and over again harmonizes with nature around him. Thereby over time, an inner refinement occurs, which is caused by an 'alignment' or 'coherence' with the natural energy of the Dao.

The Dao is, in short, inwardly felt more and more clearly and there is ultimately nothing that can undo that because the Dao Is.

Nature also likes to connect with the Daoïst, nature has nothing to fear because the Daoïst treats nature with a lot of mutual respect. You could say, the Daoïst is nature, nature is the Dao.

Unfortunately, at this time at the hands of various artificial energies and technologies, people get disturbed in their natural energy. Stress and agitation arise, restfulness is out of thought and peoples mind and there is no way of serenity and a natural environment. An increase in various diseases is resulting from these because life energy is quickly used up rather than being used in a quiet and relaxed lifestyle. People work (dabbling) for a retirement that they often will not even reach or get.

Then you would think that it could be useful to start 'retiring' as soon as possible. Retirement means as much as withdrawal or retreat. Why should you get overly stressed for years to get a retirement income, let your life pass by in a hurry, without the security of getting old anyway? Our life-force is like a battery that slowly gets empty, the fullness of the battery can determine the number of life-years of the individual human being.

In short, where the mobile phone, computer, TV, radio and game consoles dominate, there is absence of serenity. The opposite is rather true.

But the man himself is able to make choices and decisions in things he may or may not participate. What he follows or what he dismisses.

Even in a technological world, it is possible to put your focus on restoring serenity and to the renewal of your reconnection with nature which is Dao.

Therefore, we want to emphasize that Daoism is no religion, there is no belief in a visible humanized supreme being which shall act as a judiciary or punishes or rewards.

We are convinced that Lao-Tse never had the intention that images would be made of him and used to direct people to faith. Lao-Tse only had a message to his fellow human beings, wrapped in the Dao de Jing, where he would call the man of nowadays to use his common sense and think for himself.

Man is part of nature. Nature is also Consciousness and Awareness in other forms and also behaves according to the polarity forces of yin and yang. It is nature that makes its own seasonal changes and shifts. Nature is earlier than human beings, rivers and mountains have a much longer lifespan than we humans have.

However, they are also constantly changing, even in the smallest visible parts, we can see (it could be at the level of a grain of sand).

Rivers also shift their course if necessary, water always flows and always takes the easiest route by itself. Water goes around everything in its way and is able to show many forces. Water has greater physical strength than man and is able to drag the body in a stream or to flood it by a wave.

The same applies to the wind, which can show many forces that we humans cannot withstand.

We humans can not physically withstand excessive firepower, it would make us go all the way in ash and smoke.

We humans cannot withstand the forces of the earth, we are only organisms that can temporarily be fed by the things that earth produces for us. Earth is constantly subject to change and is continually adapting to changing circumstances. Actually, Earth is an organism that is able to keep all organisms miraculously together, keeps them in some way controlled by the functions which it has available.

If we humans think that we have the power over the earth, then we are mistaken. We are one of the weakest links in the entire ecosystem and we put it off against all the above-mentioned forces when it comes to it.

But earth is a very important function for us people, for it is She who feeds us and makes sure that our body can build up. All five elements (water, wood, fire, earth, and metal) build our body through all stages of growth, we are physical that, and at the end of our lives we gradually give all elements back to the earth again.

Therefore we focus on the restoration of the natural, the teachings of the polarities of yin and yang and the theory of five elements are very useful tools for that. A concise explanation of these you will find later on in this book. We do not need to reinvent the wheel, but we should remind again what is natural and what is not and thereby make appropriate choices. We are not only doing this for ourselves but at the same time for all the organisms present in this Universe. This happens naturally because we are all interconnected from the One, even though the person usually experiences a great sense of separation by means of the artificial world as it is today.

Everybody in this world is useful and adds its parts to the sum total, both positive and negative.

The Dao teachings can help the Western man to return to its natural origin. Nature itself here is the greatest teacher, as will also appear from the various texts in the Dao De Jing and I Ching. These are two key books that help to get a greater understanding of the Dao and its workings. This is done by feeling inward what these ancient writings have to say, even if the texts speak in riddles. And even if there is only one phrase in a text that is understood during reading.

The books work through repetition, whereby every time at the right moment a new insight is revealed so that the reader can think about it and muse and solve a puzzle.

The teachings of the Dao make extensive use of comparisons with natural phenomena and involve them in organic man.

As an example we mention here the statement: "Be like water", meaning that water always adapts to the place where it is at that time and is going around things. So even if there are obstacles in a flowing river, then water always goes around it and cannot be stopped. By getting more insight into the natural phenomena, you yourself will feel what is meant by these kinds of sayings and you will actually get beautifully workable insights for human life.

The books of the great Masters, Lao-Tse and Chuang-Tse, are still very valuable guides to receive more understanding of the functioning of the Dao, the visible Universe, and to catch glimpses of the invisible, intangible and ungraspable which cannot be spoken.

The temple is in yourself, it is always with you anywhere, although most people do not recognize this anymore. We want to point out, that it is even quite possible at this time to enter the inner natural state of being again. It is an individual Way, which is not really a road because it leads to inwards and is inscrutable. There is no fixed route or designation possible because it depends a lot on personal circumstances.

In any case, every human being carries a backpack on the backfilled with all kinds of memories of past experiences, with own family patterns, with opinions of others, with opinions you have about yourself, with wishes that are cherished, with feelings, with ideas, with emotions, with fears, with uncertainties, with ballast, with "yes, but", with procrastination, with varying moods, with physical pains, with feelings of powerlessness sometimes, with frustration, with feelings of lack, with the feeling to carry the world on your shoulders equal Atlas.

Recognizable?

That can be quite a heavyweight depending on what has already been done to clear things out. But that is actually what is needed, emptying out your backpack. And then see which things in that backpack really serve for a joyful life. What are you keeping and what are you putting away? But also take a closer look whether all those opinions of 'others' have been correct, or whether it is high time to dispose them.

This begins with the letting go of all assumptions that you carry right now. Instead, the question "Is this true", "is this really so"? But also the question "Who or what am I (truly/really)"? Am I what another says I am, or is it completely different?

Dare to open your eyes and, step by step, take a closer look at all 'things' that come bubbling up from within yourself. Such as feelings about: "who am I", "what can I", "what can I not".

And if there is something bubbling inside that says: "I cannot", then be careful and look very carefully where that voice comes from. Who is it that speaks there? Is it maybe an old acquaintance from this life, that you have ever encountered anywhere and which has infected you with an opinion about yourself?

Could they be opinions from school, TV, news, other media, work, sports teachers and so on?

As soon as you start noticing that those opinions are not yours; then let them go, they are of no use at all and do not help you to progress in life but keep you small.

Make it joyful for yourself, make it like a game and above all be very loving and caring for yourself. You will start noticing that you are much more funny, sweeter, kinder, spontaneous and natural than you ever thought. And that, actually, you are many years stirring yourself up, walking on tiptoes or eggshells to meet a certain image for the outside world. A want to join yourself in the overall social success in society. A made-up fairy tale and for my part what they call "The American Dream".

Most dreams are a deception. They are also often held up to you through advertisements of idyllic places and paradises.

Nevertheless, life is the most truthful, as it has its natural course. The well-known images are meant to make you strive for improvements, accumulations, chasing after some idea or concept.

But what happens if you do not reach that? Then the bubble will burst, make an end to the illusion and then it makes you become disillusioned.

We want to show you that this is not necessary at all, that there are other ways to live a life in full satisfaction despite its simplicity and modesty.

The Universe is a sum of parts, from which all visible and invisible things have been formed. If it is about the division of the present matter, we can know logically that if accumulation happens at one place, at the same time a decrease will take place somewhere else. This is because the Universe always takes care of a natural balance for the Whole. Which happens to be the working of the polarities of yin and yang.

If there happens to be too much yang, there will come a time that polarity flips over to yin. That is a natural correction.

The polarities of yin and yang can be worked out on all worldly phenomena, as such we can also view the happenings of shocking world events as being corrections coming from that principle. That does not mean that man cannot do anything about it, it does mean that a cosmic correction takes place on human action and intervention in nature, as soon as the tipping point is reached. That may be in the form of natural disasters, could cost lives and takes place with the snap of a finger.

 As pointed out before, mankind is subordinate to the movements of nature, in so far as it is physically limited.

Concerning the Mind, Consciousness, and Awareness, other values apply because these are not physical and therefore, do not need to be affected by the laws of nature. Consciousness is energetical, it is actually (thought) waves and currents and they are actually not tangible but ethereal. They cannot be grasped, although they can sometimes take on emotionally grotesque forms and seem to manifest themselves physically (for example through pains felt in the body).

All those sensations take place in the field of movement, Consciousness, and are being registered and observed from there. That is why we speak of conscious and unconscious, for example, if you faint or collapse.

But who is it that is able to mention both sensations?

In principle, there is a temporary loss of consciousness if you faint. Yet you are conscious of it yourself, from a different capacity, that you were out of your body for a moment (what happens if you faint is that temporarily you do not feel your body, you are not there for a moment).

The One who knows to appoint this is Awareness, that is the primordial part in you that is always present, your true essence.

It is present everywhere and always, receiving everything but has no judgment. If you faint, you temporarily fall back into your source/essence (Awareness) and as soon as you recover, you return again from that into your body (Consciousness).

Consciousness is an infinite field of information, too big to comprehend for the individual mind, it stores all information of the whole manifestation (sum total) in the energetical form (which is not visible). What we see, hear, taste, sense, smell on this earth plane is a projection of this energy field (infinite field of information).

Therefore the individual cannot clearly decide what would be useful for the whole. It is already difficult enough to make the right choice for 100%, taking into account the immediate circumstances in your own environment. We do not know the consequences of our choices directly, we can only suspect them and let time show whether we have acted correctly.

Seen from this knowledge, we can also state that it is impossible for people who are leading, to come up with the right solutions for tribes, larger areas, and major issues. In fact, we can cautiously draw the conclusion that they, just like all of us, can only choose for their personal interests.

And actually, as an individual you can see that you are completely dependent on yourself, you bear responsibility for your own life and therefore must be careful that you yourself remain alive.

The old fashioned model of survival of the fittest is still accurate and present in this world.

A mouse will never beat a lion. That is why it is necessary for you to develop the power of a lion for the sake of your own survival. And that starts on the mental plane, it starts with your individual energy and energy field.

Right now you may have a life that seems to be completely in order, that you have everything at hand, financial as well as material and social. Still, this can flip to the opposite if the circumstances in your environment change, something like this is called an (energetical) landslide.

That is why a majority of people is stressed out, they need to take more and more actions and try to keep dishes in the air to keep their lives the way it is now. Actually, the booster is fear of material loss. And actually, it is very fair to say that that fear is right.

On the other hand, it can also be time to take a good look at it, what is matter and what does it yield, what does it cost, what is it worth to you?

Everything you have ensures that you have to worry more, lose more energy on 'things' with a lot of stress, while you could also enjoy a restful life without stress.

The only question you need to ask yourself is: Am I aware? Am I aware of my doings, my life and everything that is interwoven with it?

Just make a personal balance and then take a good look at the weight you carry in your backpack. You may ask yourself if you are really satisfied and happy with that. What do you have to do and not do to keep it? And is everything you think you possess really permanent? Just take a closer look at which is permanently retained and what is temporary here.

And maybe you come to these questions in such a way that you decide you want to do it differently for yourself.

Is it not a fair question when it comes to your life? You have been given your life as a person to experience that which is important to you, what you like to experience, to do the things you enjoy.

We were born here for life, to enjoy life, but are we really doing that?

Or are we, humans, with all our hurry and stress only living to die?

We find this a question that is worth asking.

If this question is on your agenda as well, you are right on track. If not, it could be time for some changes you can start to make for yourself.

As we mentioned before, there is an interaction between energy and attention. But it also happens to be, that the individual inner energy has a decent influence on personal life. If you start working with this for yourself, changes in your life may start to occur in a positive way and can start to direct your life in a positive turn. But also it will become clear which people, things and affairs will suit you best personally and in a natural way.

From the teachings of the Dao, Dao De Jing and I Ching, you can receive personal insights that help you to develop yourself and your understanding. It will gradually help you to connect more deeply with your inner nature, with nature itself and with that what lies at everyone's origin.

A new world may open up for you.

We encourage you to inquire for yourself if the information we point out here is workable for you personally. We gathered all sorts of basic knowledge from the teachings of the Dao, which is only a starting point for your individual inquiry.

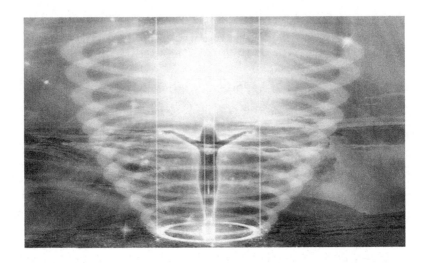

Chi

The meaning of the word 'Chi' (also Qi) in Chinese is energy or life-force.

Everything around us is energy and all energy is (visible and invisible) connected with each other as One/Unity (Dao). When around 2500 BC the Dao De Jing was recorded by Lao-Tse, there must have been an opening in Consciousness/Awareness through which knowledge concerning the energetical functioning (Consciousness/Awareness) of this Universe could seep through.

Yin and Yang

In any case, in the above period of time, the functioning of the polarity of yin and yang has been recorded and what it means for the functioning of all organisms in the Universe. It is a balancing dynamic which is active in all forms, where rest and movement fluctuate continuously.

But at the same time, in each side/part, everything else is potentially present at the same time (that is why you see the dots in the symbol), in a continuous variety of opposites. Nothing is fully yin or fully yang. The polarity forces are always related to each other and cannot exist without each other. They happen to be relative and not absolute.

If a man is able to understand this polarity, uses it as a tool to be able to see the successive changes, then the principle of yin and yang can be applied to help us balancing and harmonizing our lives.

It is certainly worth enquiring on this polarity and doing research on the topic, it is a principle which is logically explainable (action-reaction).

At the back of this book, you will find a practical addition to inquire on the dynamics of this polarity for yourself.

Life-force

In all organisms, before birth, there is an energetical germ (chi) in which a potential is stored for a time span of life which is unique for every being. From the perspective of Western concepts, we might name it DNA.

We could imagine our 'germ' as that which may germinate and may come to blossom in a natural way.

To fulfill that process, energy is used from the germ and transferred into vigor and creation, which we hopefully use for ourselves in the right way so that we can enjoy it for a long time.

We are the ones who can and should make choices about how and what we spend our energy on. But who is aware of this in the present time of hurrying and chasing?

How consciously do you live? What do you spend your time on? Do you really do the things you enjoy? Do you live from your inner core (your true potential is stored in there, which means also your life-goals)? How well do you listen to your inner voice (or do you let others determine for you every time)? Are you sufficiently at rest or do you feel hunted and/or stressed?

These are all questions that you may ask yourself to be able to return to your natural inner essence, which lays deep inside yourself and where you can reconnect with yourself.

In the end, we are all, without exception, subject to a certain degree of decay and as soon as the individual life-force is over then our body will stop its functioning.

This is a natural process that we see everywhere in nature, we people are not different from trees, plants, flowers, animals and other organisms. Even earth is prone to fluctuate forces and influences of all living beings. Mother earth is a balancing force, she always tries to restore and harmonize all of our excesses over and over and has her own ways for that.

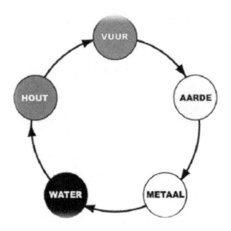

5 Elements

Water, wood, fire, earth, and metal are the elements that construct everything on our earth. So we humans live under the influence of the elements, our body is built out of it and these elements interact with all other organisms in our environment.

Each element has its own characteristics and qualities, which we could use to balance and harmonize ourselves. But this subject requires a more deepening inquiry and understanding.

If we consciously start working together with all the above-mentioned factors, then we can come to a harmonious whole and even in alignment with the Dao (Awareness).

Dao is harmony, balance, peace, and love

Dao is chi

Dao is in all

All are in Dao

Still, Dao is invisible and intangible because it is infinite and unbounded, while the individual lacks the brain capacity to understand the wholeness of All.

The individual only knows that 'part' of Dao he is as himself, and where he himself can start inwardly to connect with and maintain an inner connection. It finds itself as a loving presence in the deepest core of our being and opens up from silence if we allow that to happen ourselves.

For that, it is not necessary to retreat in a cave or to perform all kinds of other actions. The only thing asked from us is, despite all challenges in this era, to direct our focus and attention at 'emptying ourselves out' with regards to our convictions and assumptions. It asks us to return to our original state of being, the state of a newborn baby which never has spoken and has not yet formed an opinion about this world. It asks from us to let go of past as well as future and to completely surrender to the present. In such a way that we become connected to our true nature again, which knows no fear of change but knows how to adapt flawlessly and spontaneously to all circumstances.

Below is a quote from the Dao De Jing. Daoism regularly uses short recorded texts and parables that have the ability to penetrate the (deeper) consciousness of the reader.

The ego is a monkey catapulting through the jungle:

Totally fascinated by the realm of the senses,

it swings from one desire to the next,

one conflict to the next,

one self-centered idea to the next.

If you threaten it, it actually fears for its life.

Let this monkey go.

Let the senses go.

Let desires go.

Let conflicts go.

Let ideas go.

Let the fiction of life and death go.

Just remain in the center, watching.

And then forget that you are there.

From: The Unknown Teachings of Lao Tzu/Hua Hu Ching/by Brian Walker

A newborn baby looks with innocent eyes into the wide world and observes without judgment.

But who or what is it that looks through those eyes? Where was this baby before the light of life was seen and before there was any conception?

We can ask a similar pair of questions when it comes to the end of life.

Who or what is it that looks through the eyes of the dying? Who or what is it who knows about a body and all the sensations that are felt in it? And who or what is it that is aware of letting go of a body and of the 10.000 things that this earth encompasses?

Is there actually a birth and/or death? Or do we have the privilege of going through several stages and are we all engaged in a continuous process of consciousness-transformation?

Breathing

The very first activity when we are born: Breathing!

Our lungs blow open as soon as we breathe in our first air, the life-journey of the body is started. Breathing is automatically regulated by our nervous system but can deviate from the natural rhythm by circumstances.

There are in any case a number of factors that can have a disruptive influence on the "natural relaxed (deep abdominal) breathing".

Stress is one of the main causes of this in these times and the underlying emotion is usually fear. The result is that breathing becomes shallower and as a result stays higher on the chest, the in- and out-breaths become shorter and less oxygen enters the body. As a result, the feeling of stress in the body increases, it gives you a feeling of excitement without being able to find an identifiable cause for it, and you can end up in a vicious circle. The same effect is generated by long-term attention or identification with things outside yourself. Especially the influence of working with screens and the processing of increasing external information-flows in various media is enormous.

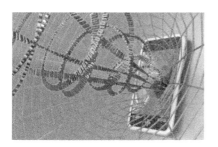 

It seems that all kinds of information come our way, the reality is that we get caught in a web and that our energy is sucked into the device.

Are you aware of this?

As soon as you are behind a screen, your eyes bring your attention to other things and you actually forget your body and your breathing starts to react to the things you see. You can also notice this when someone starts to talk to you, you usually do not hear immediately what someone else is saying. That person must first, as it were, wake you up. While you are immersed in the things that pass by on your screen, your breathing also changes at the same time. Especially when there are exciting things to see, which awaken in your body a sensation of tension and stress.

Pay attention to this for yourself, watch and feel what happens if you use the "natural relaxed (deep abdominal) breathing" so that you get to know your own body reactions very well.

Are you aware of your breathing? Is your breathing directed deep into the lower abdomen, or are you (too) high in the chest with your breathing?

If that is the case, then take a seat to calm yourself down and follow your breaths and lead them back deeper and deeper into the lower abdomen. It is important for a pleasant functioning for yourself, that breathing remains natural. There are also exercises that we will work out in a separate online module.

Breathing is arranged so naturally that it happens that you blow your last breath when your body function ends at the end of your life. Then air (ether) is given back to where it originally came from. Because this too is 'chi'.

Body – Mind

A body that is (naturally) well-nourished contributes to a balanced functioning of the mind. The reverse is also the case, that a well-nourished mind from balance and rest has a positive effect on the body.

Both are complementary to each other and need each other for a nice and vital life.

A refined harmonization between body and mind contribute to good chi, or "good spirit".

Traditional Chinese Medicine (TCM)

According to Traditional Chinese Medicine, a doctor is educated to be a physician who accompanies man during his life to stay healthy. Prevention plays a very important role in this, it prevents people from becoming ill and thus ensuring that they remain as vital as possible.

In the West are also Chinese physicians who have been trained according to the TCM and acupuncture. They often work with herbal compositions for support and have a range of other treatment methods that they use to work on the body's energy system. We do not work these methods any further in this book, but only mention it so you know that this is the official healing and treatment method in China.

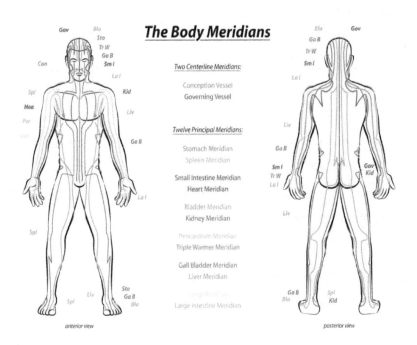

The Body Meridians

Two Centerline Meridians:

Conception Vessel
Governing Vessel

Twelve Principal Meridians:

Stomach Meridian
Spleen Meridian

Small Intestine Meridian
Heart Meridian

Bladder Meridian
Kidney Meridian

Pericardium Meridian
Triple Warmer Meridian

Gall Bladder Meridian
Liver Meridian

Lung Meridian
Large Intestine Meridian

anterior view

posterior view

Meridians (energy channels)

Chinese medicine is based on the optimal functioning and balancing of the body through optimal flow in the energy channels (meridians) in the body. Each organ has its own energy course, it has its own operating time on the day and works according to a precise system together with other organs.

41

Both hands and feet have meridian points (reflex-points) and there are many laying scattered all over the body. These can be used in acupressure or acupuncture if there is a poor flow in the energy channel (meridian).

The intention is that our energy continues to flow optimally so that the organs continue to function as optimally as possible.

It is important for health and wellbeing that the energy channels remain open, the life-energy can be optimally used and the body is burdened as little as possible with its various vital functions.

Walking daily, for a minimum of 30 minutes, is important for the flow in the energy channels. Under the feet are several energy points that are stimulated during the walk and help to keep the energy channels open.

In addition, the consciously executed forms of movement of Chi-Dao Qigong are a very good support for our 'power plant'.

Qigong

Qigong (and also Tai Chi) have been used since the old days in everyday life to support the vitality of a man. In China, one has been able to establish that Qigong can have a preventive effect that is working on the more delicate energies of the body. As Qigong is practiced frequently and for a long time, the various energy flows in the body will become better attuned to each other. For the practitioner, observable changes can occur both inwardly and in alignment with the environment.

A normal sports practice goes without the 'conscious use' of our conscious mind. Qigong uses the conscious mind for the purpose of following movements/chi and refining them. You are constantly paying attention to the movements while you are performing the movements, and the mind does not have to keep an eye on other practical actions such as your personal safety during ballgames or weightlifting.

Nowadays we see more and more that Qigong and Tai Chi is practiced with the use of the media without good personal guidance. A warning is certainly appropriate in this. These forms of movement are traditionally transferred from master to pupil in Asian countries (and increasingly in the West) and not through the media. Why this is, has to do with painful consequences that you can experience physically and mentally over time. The master who teaches you Qigong or Tai Chi (no matter what form) keeps a close eye on whether you perform the movements correctly to prevent damage to your body, and corrects where it is necessary. But who corrects you if you try to learn it via media or DVD?

Chi-Dao

Chi-Full team has developed Chi-Dao Qigong, which is suitable for the challenges of this time. It is a delicate form of movement in which stress release is central so that the refined inner energies can be observed individually again. Chi-Dao is meant to stimulate a personal growth of consciousness from rest. It is not necessary to be an athlete or to have a great condition and suppleness. Chi-Dao brings each individual what is needed at the moment.

Practicing Chi-Dao brings the practitioner back into contact with the natural chi currents so that the original vitality can show itself again. Our original energy (peace, balance, harmony) will automatically become visible as we can release more inner ballast.

In the case of medical issues, we always recommend consulting a medical professional.

Meditation

Meditation is primarily intended to bring body and mind in balance through rest.

We, humans, are so busy with our activities of all day, where the mind turns overtime and jumps from the heel onto the branch, that it has become a habit to say to others 'I am busy'.

Consciously making time to unwind using various methods, is what gives you a lot of personal insights without having to be instantly 'vague'.

Meditation does not happen with the intention of all kinds of fantastic (dream) experiences but is focused on the coming to a standstill of the mind after a while. Therefore there is meditation on silence, emptiness and actually nothingness. For many people this sounds frightening, but it is not. In fact, every new idea springs from silence again and again and that is a natural state of being.

People confuse all ever faster jumps of the mind, by the Daoïst also called monkey mind, as a mind that works at full speed and successfully. On the other hand, they do not realize that the mind uses a lot of life-energy to produce a lot of nonsensical thoughts and is actually on the way to making people mentally ill. Consequences of an over-stimulated mind include excessive stress, overstrain, burn out and from these arise many physical complaints and other unwanted issues. We work from the teachings of the Dao with Zuowang Lun meditation and can also teach you how to do this.

The body

Seen from the Chinese perspective, our physical body is an energetical body that can give a multiplicity of signals, from gross to very subtle, inwardly as well as outwardly.

In this book, we will not go into this subject too deeply, because we focus on gaining a different view of the human body and adapting the lifestyle to a more energy-oriented vision.

We intend to make you more aware and help you to consciously apply this knowledge to yourself. It will take some getting used to, but awareness in this can grow and it will become more and more fun to experience how the body is actually tuned (or aligned).

Our bits of advice may be read from the individual building up of Good Chi, to become connected to the natural energy (Dao) we originate from.

We ask you to look at the topics below from a different angle and to start paying attention to them in your daily life. See for yourself what these things mean for you in your daily life and whether it will be helpful for you to make some adjustments. It is a matter of trying and being guided by your inner feelings.

(Night)rest

A good night's sleep requires a lot of preparation from the Daoïst way of life.

First of all, a switch is made quickly to the rest of the body after the evening meal. No more study activities are being undertaken, the mind is also being led to a quiet movement.

Well before 23.00 hours, the body is laid to rest so that important organ processes can take place in rest. The gallbladder is active with the production of bile from 23.00 hours. Then the liver starts from 01.00 hours to take over the detoxification process and remove bulking matter (toxins) from the body.

During the night hours, the body regenerates and rejuvenation takes place.

If the mind is put in a relaxed mood well before sleep time, the body will also relax and surrender easily to sleep.

Walking/hiking

We cannot emphasize enough to walk every day for at least 30 minutes (longer is also allowed, of course) in a normal quiet pace so that the energy points under the feet are massaged and can contribute to a good circulation in the body. As we walk, we help our body to eliminate toxins and we ensure that our energy channels remain open.

If we are functioning optimally, energy flows through us like a river without blockages.

In our busy world (manifestation), which is mainly characterized as yang (fast and speedy action/movement) in this time, we do not need any more rush or busy moments. If the polarity gets too extreme in one part of the yin-yang symbol, then we can compensate and balance it by living more to the contrary (in this case it will be more a yin-energy, slow and tranquil action/movement).

If you simply relax and move in a calm mood will be sufficient to refresh and recover yourself completely. Too many busy or performance-oriented activities only contribute to an increase in stress, resulting in a decrease of life force.

While walking you can try to breathe to the rhythm of your steps. For example, with the attention, you breathe in during 4 steps and breathe out during 4 steps. You can make adjustments to what feels best for you, by choosing more or fewer steps. The amount of steps has nothing to do with performance, it has to feel pleasant and feels comfortable for your body. After a while you can start to feel like you're walking on clouds and you might find that you can walk longer distances without getting tired. This was widely used in China in earlier times.

Water

The human body consists of water for 70%. That is why it is important to refresh our water management for a natural balance in our body, with the purest and highest quality of water.

Water contributes, through the kidneys, to the excretion of waste substances from our body and is a must in this current time.

However, it is not the intention to refuel water continuously during the day, drink when you are thirsty and each time refill yourself until the feeling of thirst is gone.

Drinking water continuously is more of a burden on the kidneys and can cause other complaints.

Nutrition/food

From the perspective of our energetical body, it is important to prepare the highest quality of food from natural products. With that we mean, vegetables, fruits, nuts, seeds, plants and herbs, which carry a high level 'energy frequency' and can help us to recharge our body.

Everything is energy and has its own energetical vibration/frequency, that is how we can at the same time distinguish between food with a high energy value and food with a low energy value. Pure and natural foods provide us with good chi for our body. And it even matters who prepare our food and how hopefully in a relaxed manner and in a good mood. That gives us the best refreshing and constructive meal that we can wish for.

Our hands are full of energy(points). And intentions and states of mind flow through both our body as well as our hands. We are able to transfer energy through our hands to our environment, including our food.

The best food is prepared in Good Chi, which means the highest vibration/frequency of love (peace, balance, and harmony).

We have no guarantee where our fruits, vegetables, seeds, and nuts are grown. We could not know (except if we eat from our own garden), but we can choose the best nutrition/food for ourselves and others.

We advise you to wash fruit and vegetables in warm water with a dash of vinegar during this time (due to environmental issues). Leave them there for a few minutes and then rinse them well with water to remove any toxic substances as much as possible. You will also notice that the flavors of fruit and vegetables will become more refined.

If you decide to change your eating habits and start eating natural, your energetic frequency will also increase because your body and mind feel much better in Good Chi.

We invite you to get started to experience for yourself what it does for you. If you want to find more information about this, then you can check out more info on food or cooking according to the 5 elements. This covers a very extensive area and focuses on individual energy requirements. This method is even suitable for dealing with various individual health problems.

Balance

Our body is a complex functioning whole in which all organs work together and also all bodily functions are accurately regulated.

This can sometimes be disrupted due to various causes, causing the body to become unbalanced. It may even be that a literal 'inclination' will occur due to altered muscle tension in one or several muscles in the body.

The body itself does everything first instance to correct and heal itself.

The better we are tuned to the subtler (energetical) signals of our body, the sooner we can take preventive measures by ourselves to prevent inconveniences.

A number of these preventive measures are already mentioned in this book. These can be used entirely by study and practical exercise and will contribute to personal development and growth. All the time spent on this is more than compensated by an increasing balance in body-mind and spirit.

Coherence

By coherence, we mean life in accordance with the lifestream both inside ourselves and in the outside world. We have no individual control over what happens in the outside world, life brings us situations that we have to face. And we individually have a choice what we do with those situations.

The concept of the polarity of yin and yang can help us to see the various successive action-response patterns. The more we are in the present, the more focus and concentration we have. By letting go of the past and the future, we can see every moment as fresh and free ourselves from stress.

A person is and remains mainly healthy because of his own natural vitality. Any remedial method, herbs or medication, works by removing an external attacker or toxins created in the body.

Encouraging people to take care of their own recovery by strengthening and maintaining their natural vitality, so that the body continues to function healthy, is our goal.

95% of all illnesses are healed by the power of man himself, only 5% heals through the treatment. An integrated approach prevents misery, that is an organic and holistic approach to life itself.

A natural vitality is the source of self-healing.

If vitality in a person is low the various practices work, together with a number of important lifestyle changes, to build renewed vitality and at the same time, a health issue may start to solve itself. This is a long way and requires daily attention and self-care from the individual. We speak of a healthy person when there is 100% vitality. If someone is ill, the flow of energy in the energy channels is blocked or weakened.

Temperature regulation

In cold (yin) countries people need more exercise. In warm (yang) countries people benefit more from rest.

Overpopulation (yang) is currently the biggest reason for the onset of aggression, especially when the temperatures are rising and people continue to rush and chase. Then a yang excess develops which means that more yang heat is created in the body and more rest has to be taken to ensure cooling (yin) so that the body processes (and also mental processes) can normalize again. Normalizing actually means that you 'walk in the middle' and stay away from the extremities.

Therefore it is important to avoid overstimulation and overactivity in summer (or tropical climate).

If you feel cold in your body, you can regulate your own temperature by making your mouth round and puffing out your breath in 3 short breathings out.

If you feel the heat in your body, you can regulate your temperature by making your mouth wide open and puffing out 7, 21 or 36 times 'Kau'-sound while breathing out. You will literally breathe out the heat from your body.

Sweating

If you are sweating too much, you will lose energy and sooner catch a cold. If you have too little energy, then you become vulnerable to an invasion of the worst energies.

Water in your body can also be toxic, peeing too often can weaken.

Sweating and peeing regulate the fluid balance in your body.

A good key to the fluid balance is how much you drink, what you drink and when you drink.

Preferably you drink water 50/50, hot/cold mixture, yin and yang in balance. The body then has to work least to absorb the water and that saves energy.

Sleeping

You do not want to sleep continuously in the same position but change this regularly. It is important to go to sleep completely relaxed and peaceful. Do not eat before going to sleep, digestion than will be at ease and food will not be fermenting in the stomach. If you go to sleep relaxed and at ease, it also prevents bad dreams.

If you want to get to know your original energy, it is important to cultivate energy. This means that for every action you first prepare yourself well, especially as much as possible you relax and release tension, and thus collect good energy. This allows you to strengthen the connection with your natural inner energy.

Good energy means that you are well equipped, consuming good healthy food and doing nothing 'over the top'.

Never sleep with your head North in connection with polarity (magnetism). South, West or East is the best, those are the directions that are most favorable to the energy of the Sun. The wrong direction to sleep is to force your rhythm because you don't lay your body to rest in optimally quiet and tranquil energy.

Energy

Talking about energy and explaining exactly what it is, is actually an impossible task. This is because energy is ungraspable and intangible, however, it is felt individually. It depends also on the individual attunement whether and in which way energy is observed. Energy can show itself in varying degrees, from very dense and heavy to very subtle, refined and light. It is the senses that can perceive it, without senses nothing happens.

We mention here some examples, the weather, the season, atmosphere, people, animals, sounds, scents, tastes. These are all things that are present, visible as well as invisible.

Talking about energy is difficult because this is individually perceived so variable. One person signals something, the other person does not signal something. We are not going deeper into this, we only want to point out to you that the enhancement and refinement of your perception can only develop individually. It is not advisable to force this process, it follows a gradual path as your insights change over time.

We take the sun as an example, a radiant sunny and warm day, where one person loves the warmth while the other person finds the warmth disturbing. These are differences in perception and awareness. They are respected in all ways because each person is 'stringed' in their own way.

If you are sensitive to 'energy', then you will most likely experience a lot of subtle energy from your surroundings. You register everything you perceive within yourself, which is the place where the information is processed and stored. This also happens unnoticed, for example, if you have been in places where there are many different people.

That's why we focus on getting and keeping the individual energy field in order and balanced.

Keeping your energy optimal is done by keeping your body and mind together. That means that you cannot leave your mind (thoughts) away from your body too far and also not too long. You keep feeling with the signals your body produces and as soon as you better control that skill you will even be able to notice the smallest details.

Within the teachings of the Dao, Body-Mind-Spirit is also named the 3 partners. These 3 cans, if they are well balanced and harmonized, reach unity together because the connection with the inner natural energy can be restored completely. Then, there is no longer any fragmentation but a sense of wholeness and completeness. We may also call this a magical balance.

Again, we have tried to describe a number of facets for the purpose of broadening the understanding of the reader. But actually, we can only say, discover this completely for yourself if you want to know more about this or if you want to develop this for yourself. You will have to invent this completely within yourself, there is nobody who can do this for you.

The Integral Way

The way of the Dao is also called "the integral way" and means that you are willing to follow the lifestream entirely (Dao), which means a kind of surrender or 'Wu-Wei'. This goes out before all forms of religion and ideology and has to do with taking part in life itself from direct experience and being present regardless of the workings you encounter on your way. The best possible cooperation with the organic whole is involved here.

It is very broad teaching in which all 3 partners (body-mind-spirit) are brought together in natural balance and harmony by working daily on the subject with focus and attention. The various practices, such as meditation, Qigong and an adaptation of lifestyle, contribute to a change in the inner energy flows and can gradually lead to inner equilibrium.

When we talk about spirit, then we mean the natural inner self, the 'being-so-of-itself'.

The integral path is actually a 'middle way' in which we do not punish the Ego and physical body but make use of it in the right way. There is no question of asceticism, the body is not punished, there is not being walked into a loin cloth and it is not starved, but of a way of simplicity and simplification. If we were to speak in terms of this modern age, you could say that we are discarding all the over-stimulating and artificial things in this world. That we take a closer look at our lives and return inwardly to our natural inner state of being.

This is not visible on the outside, but it can be felt deep inside ourselves.

Extremes are not natural and we cannot deny physical life. But we can regulate it.

Universal Mind

The universal predisposition of our minds involves the power of nature to restore its own condition and health, and return to a normal state of being after a regional disaster. What happens in nature, is the same as what happens in the human body.

Spirit

The spirit is the essential energy of the universe and is the infinite energy that we people cannot comprehend with our body-mind. It is an extension of heavenly energy, just as our hand is an extension of our body. Each individual is essentially an extension of the Universe (Consciousness) and fulfills an organic role.

The function of the mind is an integration of yin and yang (cerebral hemispheres) and is intended to maintain our existence (life).

Sun energy = action + doing

Moon Energy = reflection + resistance

Superficially, these two energies are different, nevertheless, they are still one energy because they both find their origins in the One (Awareness/Dao). The One (Awareness/Dao) is the unidentifiable, indescribable, intangible, infinite origin of all things.

Sun and Moon are therefore a result from the One in 2 (Yang and Yin).

5 Universal Virtues

These are 5 energies that together form a cycle, a set of 5 phases.

Virtues are the more refined functions (higher moral standard) of the spirit or more subtle functions of nature.

There are 3 cycles that affect the Earth, the annual solar cycle, the monthly lunar cycle, and the daily earth cycle. These form our natural environment and reflect themselves inwardly in each individual.

The annual solar cycle consists of 5 parts:

1. Spring, reflects positive energy and regeneration

2. Summer, time of full growth

3. Autumn, contraction, and withdrawal of heat

4. Winter, the heat of the surface sinks deep into the earth and back into the life Force (germ) and stores itself therein

These 4 phases of the solar cycle are an expression of every movement of life on Earth.

5. Earth, produces its own energy so that the energy from the cosmos/sky is harmonized.

The monthly lunar cycle, also known as the White Route, consists of 28 lunar states, each night showing a different constellation (composition).

The daily earth cycle concerns the rotation of the earth in which various creations appear such as the emergence of the sun, movements of the air (clouds, etc), the sinking down of the sun, etc.

The 5 universal virtues are actually the 5 energies that are present in the spirit of man, the human inner nature.

It is the 5 inner virtues that express themselves precisely in humans, as the natural energy (Dao) expresses itself.

These 5 inner virtues are:

1. Kindness/Love, whose energy is linked to spring-growth (wood) as a positive form of expression.

The negative/extreme form of expression is a weakness.

2. Rite/Manner/civilization, whose energy is linked to the summer (fire) as a positive form of expression.

The negative/extreme form of expression is superficiality.

3. Properness/uprightness, the energy of which is linked with autumn, the formable and deformable (metal) as a positive form of expression.

The negative/extreme form of expression is without principles.

4. Wisdom, whose energy is linked to winter (water) as a positive form of expression.

The negative/extreme form of expression is cold-heartedness.

5. Honesty/earnestness/faithfulness, of which the energy is linked to the earth and which is a stage of transition of all 1 to 4 as a positive form of expression. These are the 4 different energies of the entire earth cycle.

The negative/extreme form of expression is stubbornness, inflexibility.

Our 'divine' and 'masterly' energies, the natural and virtuous energies, lay in our 'center' or the 'core' of our being. In the inner center of our being, there is no question of an excessively positive or negative, there you are harmoniously and centered.

If all 5 values are practiced, understood and balanced, the result is a neutral expression. If all 5 values work together, the natural Harmony (complete truth) can be created. All 5 values are an expression of the One, positive nature of the universe.

Most teachings and teachers tend towards a highlighting of 1 virtue, causing a dramatic effect of excess on a single direction. Therefore, the expression from the natural inner beings core cannot be completed.

Our natural reality is universal, knows no divisions and is broad teaching. It encompasses everything, which means that it applies to every organism in this universe.

Learn to keep your inner nature in balance, at the right time, in the right amount, in all circumstances and situations.

In doing so, you get to know the 3 (partners) energies in yourself well, scattered energies (including by conditioning) will be returned to where they came from. By doing so, you will cherish your life energy.

When good energies are gathered by a person, life becomes a small model of 'God '.

You don't have to seek endlessly outside yourself to find a place where you can 'put away' your life or to organize your mind. You are here and now present with all 3 energies and the potential of a small ' God '.

You should respect your life, not waste it or disperse it.

If you practice the 5 values from within under all circumstances and life situations, you will step by step develop yourself and learn more about life itself. You will gradually gain access to your deeper knowledge and skills that will benefit your life and the lives of other people. That is a good basis for living in Good Chi.

Seeing your own mistakes is a sign that your true knowing or knowledge about life grows and that the light of your inner nature becomes stronger.

The two most influential elements are physical desires and the mind, it is the mind that lies between these two and is continuously moved back and forth (between past and future).

Desires come from dark energy, these usually win the battle and cause a lot of struggle and suffering.

Your inner true nature is the light in you and thus a kind of 'divine messenger'. The recognition of this is formed by intention, insight, and practice, by continuously keeping your focus and attention with it.

The inner light is always challenged and tested by external circumstances in daily life and by the so-called partners/faculties of the body-mind. The inner light is exactly in the center of your life/being and only a developed life has realized this.

The mind is the most developed area during life because from birth all attention has been focused on the successful development of yourself as a person (Ego) in the world, which is why it is the mind that now needs to turn around and help us to reregulate physical life. The mind is usually focused on chasing things outside of ourselves, but can also reverse itself at some point and take the road back inside. Then the mind, as soon as he gets exhausted from new ideas in the outside world, goes looking for his own origins. We also call this self-inquiry or self-examination.

The secret of inner cultivation is "don't let the light of your inner true nature get extinguished by the power of the dark inside yourself or outside yourself". This means that you remain in your own power despite the negativity. Let the light of your inner true nature grow.

Religions promise that, if you conform to certain conditions, you will be able to enter heaven or paradise after this life. There is a 'person/God' who judges and determines you.

In fact, there is no authority, the energy/light/spark in the core/center of your own being is All That Is. That is your natural power source, impartially present, and just observing what you experience. This center is absolute peace and balance and always present, wherever you go. This center stays small for many, without ever knowing that you can make it/this energy grow. That's what we call 'cultivating in full consciousness'. Learning new natural patterns is part of that. With that, you can decide about participating in anything for yourself which mostly means staying balanced. It is you, who has got the freedom to decide in every new moment what to do or not to do. And if you know the patterns, you will be able to make the logical conclusions. The 'spark' or 'godly part' in us is always balanced and cannot be destroyed by anything. It is us, humans, who get ourselves disordered by all impressions from inside and outside of our Selves. Without impressions, we don't have context, which means without impressions the 10.000 things will stop existing.

Out of 12 energy-hours, as you can see in the picture, every 2 hours equal 1 energy-hour (this is in the Daoïst Meridian clock one full day and night). There should never be a moment your attention gets off of 'This'.

And 'This' means in terms of Qigong and Tantien, the internal center of energy/chi That means you have to learn to concentrate day and night on your inner energy centers.

This might be hard to sense in the beginning, but after time passes and you will start recognizing and following your energy consciously, refinement will occur within yourself.

Within the teachings of Dao, the attention will constantly be pointed towards different energy centers and the in our body roaming energies. When those have all been seen and controlled, the initial energy will show itself (peace, balance, and harmony).

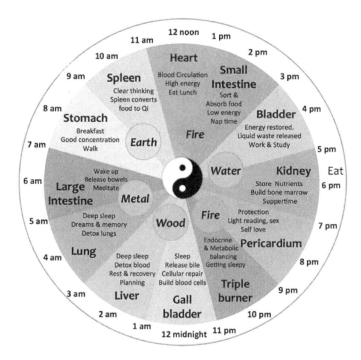

In this Meridian clock, you can see which organs will be active at what time, which activities will take place, what element they belong to and which physical activities will be best suitable and healthy at that moment.

76

3 demons

There are 3 tantiens,

1) Spirit (situated in the head) – Upper Tantien

2) Mental (situated in the mind) – Middle Tantien

3) Body (situated in the body) – Lower Tantien

In the upper Tantien (higher part) dwells the - pole desire of holding the levers of power (bossy, assertive, tyranny).

In the middle Tantien (middle part) dwells the - pole desire of possession (control, possession, wealth and prosperity).

In the lower Tantien (lower part) dwells the - pole unfulfilling desire (concerning material matters such as excessive nourishment, sexuality)

In Daoïst perspective, not being able to control these centers will prevent people from becoming Shiens, meaning free immortal spirits who are not bound to the earthly temptations. In short, when all 3 Tantiens are controlled transformation will take place inside of the human by itself.

A Shien can live on both human levels as on invisible higher energetic levels.

6 greedy thieves

The 6 greedy thieves are our senses.

1) eyes

2) ears

3) nose

4) tongue

5) body/hands

6) mind (with its different desires)

7 bloodthirsty devils

The 7 bloodthirsty devils are our emotions

1) fear, worries

2) anguish, melancholia, sadness, depression

3) shock

4) anger

5) aversion, hate

6) desire, liking

7) joy, happiness

The 6 greedy thieves, as well as the 7 bloodthirsty devils, are, according to Daoïst teachings, capable of causing physical weakness or eventually even death (for example with high blood pressure or other major illnesses).

Do you need to improve your health?

In that case, go look into the target points mentioned up above and see for yourself how they are related to your personal situation and if they need improvement.

Balance is Dao.

The highest virtue in life is Balance and Harmony.

A normal way of living is the best physician.

Calligraphy

Calligraphy is training in focus/attention and is very convenient for people with dispersed energy (who get distracted from the outside world too easily), who are not capable of organizing/mastering the movements in their mind.

Needed for calligraphy:

White paper, a brush, black ink

Or just with a stick in sand or mud

You can do this when you feel uncomfortable, to bring yourself at ease and in balance.

Symbols are pictures, which involves both the left and right side of the brain.

Calligraphy exercise connects you with your inner nature (subtle energy) and strengthens the power of the spirit.

The more often you practice, the more powerful the result.

A replacement, that you can practice anywhere, is the 'Lemniscates' (reclined 8) in a continuum with your right hand and with your left hand. When you do this, you will experience inner peace. It could be that you first have to practice this consciously, but after a while, you will notice that the movement will go more fluently.

You can practice the 'Lemniscates' movement with the mouse of your computer, with a pen on paper, with your hand on an even substrate, with your hand in the air. You can even practice the 'Lemniscates' movement with your eyes. The direction you choose to make the 'reclined 8' doesn't matter. It is all about the continued movement and the peaceful and centered effect it creates.

You practice calligraphy in a silent room, without disturbance and preferably early in the day.

Daoïst practices

There are several Daoïst practices that can contribute to repairing the natural vitality. It is mainly about pointing the individual focus and attention towards centering yourself, following the inner energy movement, and therefore sorting out your vitality over time.

Take 20 minutes/2 hours a day to harmonize and adjust your inner energy.

If you can balance your emotions, you will be freed from anger or sadness and you won't get agitated as easily anymore (because of things that happen). Emotions like anger and sadness use us up from the inside, they attack us on our individual inner energy even if we think we direct our energy on 'something' outside of ourselves. That is the treason in emotions, they are felt and noticed on the inside and there they will play themselves out. We think we are perceiving outside of ourselves because the energy will be directed towards, for example, another person. But that is an illusion. We damage ourselves through our own emotions. That is why it is so important to work on yourself and make a clean sweep within consciousness.

Immunity and a lack of immunity

A lack of immunity does not really exist. In fact, (health) issues are caused by too much resistance to things happening in life.

The phenomenon of 'immunity' needs to be explained differently. You lose a lot of energy and power because you are constantly defending yourself against influences from the outside world. You roll up your sleeves and brace yourself and, in fact, start a fight with the outer world.

In fact, you should follow the flow of life, with suppleness. Life is here to be experienced and everything will be handed to you. You don't have to look for solutions. Everything will come and go just the way it is meant to be. Even if it doesn't feel like it.

If you quit all resistance against life, everything can work/come and go through you and that is an infinite stream of things.

Don't let anyone distract or disturb you, others will fill in the exact role in your life they have to fill in. In reverse, you do the same in their lives, so they can experience too.

Don't hold on to anything but let go, there is nothing to hold on to. Everything is One movement, presence, here and now. And what is out of your sight here and now, doesn't have to be in your sight here and now. It is early enough to get moving if something shows up. No sooner than that.

Why?

Because then you will be sure it is meant for you.

Four seasons

Humans are a microcosmos of the universe, which means that everything is present in humans themselves and all we experience is at the same time a reflection of our Selves. Everything inside us moves through cyclic patterns, which are patterns we usually know as activities of our hormones.

Everything is regulated by the Law of Natural Order for every living being. The diversity in cycles is worked out in the I Ching, where they describe logical progression in different phases. If you are interested, you can read the whole I Ching from beginning to end. It is not easy to read because it is written through a lot of metaphors, but the book works on resonance so you can read it for many years while you can still discover 'something new' every time. What you read usually applies to yourself at the moment, every moment fresh and new, the I Ching can become your travel partner.

All processes flow through the same route: birth, growth, maturation, harvesting, storing.

Seen from our human life perspective, we are **born** with a fresh amount of life energy 'Chi', that is given us to **grow** and to live through life experiences. During our life journey, we plant a diversity of seeds, that will **mature** over time and will eventually start to blossom, to get ready to be **harvested**. After harvesting, we can finish by **storing** them up, so we can use them to form new energy.

It is needed and means a lot to be able to adjust yourself to every circumstance if you want to live a comfortable life. A comfortable life is mainly life in good health, our body is given to us for this one lifetime and is determining for our wellbeing.

In fact, the principles mentioned above apply to all organisms in the universe, it describes the effect of nature on humans and the response of humans on nature. If humans abstain from artificial things and live pure naturally. In short, humans and nature are connected indissolubly and are constantly interacting and exchanging.

The theory of polarities of yin and yang and the 5 elements describe the natural transformation of energy in the human body and the universe.

Herbs

Within the Traditional Chinese Medicine (TCM) a lot of herbal formulas are available and are used by Chinese physicians. There are special formulas and combinations for general and specific matters and can also help people to adjust and adapt to nature. Chemical remedies are usually isolated substances, more toxic, and the results are often a burden to other parts of the body. They are not natural and therefore odd to the body.

In nature, every organism originally is a whole with all its parts, because everything wants to be in balance and strives towards that. Natural substances are usually neutralizing and synergetic. Synergy means the benefit of the whole that will occur when all parts come together, relative to the sum of parts. In general, this means that it adds to the whole.

Natural factors and the human body

The following natural factors are influencing the human body, according to Chinese Medicine.

1. Change of season determines our biological clock and works with what they call 'the circadian rhythm'. It works through the organ clock, that has and shows a predictable cycle of chemical and physical changes in the body. These are effective on the functioning of the organs, influence moods and regulate the metabolic system.

2. Metabolism forms the whole of processes of assimilation of food in the cells of a body.

3. Sleep has a regenerating effect. We need it so all our body processes can take place in rest.

4. Breathing is an important factor; proper breathing brings a healthy energy flow into motion.

Major changes in energy can make someone vulnerable to illness and imbalance.

There are 4 seasons (winter, spring, summer, autumn) and 1 transitional season (Indian summer, which is a transitional season between summer and autumn that sometimes makes it seem like summer is extended for a little while).

Imbalance in the 5 elements in the body usually causes physical and/or emotional disturbance. Every element is connected to an organ-pair and every organ-pair is influenced throughout the season where it belongs to.

Season – organ-pair – element

Spring, liver/gallbladder, the wood element

Summer, heart/large intestine, the fire element

Indian summer, spleen/stomach, the earth element

Autumn, lung/small intestine, the metal element

Winter, kidney/bladder, the water element

The power of self-healing

We explained the bigger picture in this book, to hand you a tool to work on your own vitality.

It is important to take the very first step when a problem or weakness is still small. This means that a profound connection with your inner nature is necessary so you can easily pick up the small signals.

Unfortunately, people often only get interested in taking their health in their own hands when they already have a problem.

In fact, there are 2 steps to take:

1. Make sure your 'problem' gets healed

2. Improve your health by exercises and a proper diet (natural nutrition)

Therefore, you direct yourself towards complete recovery in a natural way. By working on your personal points of attention, you will get more and more aware of which measures are needed for your personal body-mind. These can, among other things, be found in the areas mentioned in this book.

In Western culture, acute illnesses will always be referred to a general medical practitioner or specialist who always will decide what acute medical treatment is needed.

91

We are obligated to inform people about this, even though we want to underline that humans have healing qualities by themselves and that they are accessible to everyone.

What we are talking about in this book, is a preventive solution for your physical, mental and spiritual wellbeing so you can prevent your condition and health from deterioration.

Self-healing takes place on 3 levels, body – mind – spirit, where all levels are connected. Each part has its own specific function.

Mind

Make sure you call your mind to order, that you get centered instead of letting your attention drift away. If you are capable of generating positive energy, you will start feeling freer.

We are all born the same (baby) and are able to learn how to use this primary energy again.

This starts with self-respect, self-confidence, and means that you stop believing negative things others tell you. Insecurity eats from your life-energy, like some sort of acid.

A general life standard will help the most, not too high and not too low, just following the middle ground.

If you experience psychological, mental or emotional issues, you don't know how to keep yourself balanced yet. This often means that you never put enough effort in this area of life because you didn't feel like you were worth it or because you thought someone else is better than you. You don't even like working on yourself due to these causes.

If you feel like you are unworthy, it feels like you are walking with sand (a burden) in your shoes and that takes a lot of energy.

Clear up the things that bother you, from the inside and outside! You can organize your issues by self-inquiry. How you do this, we describe in the added supplements in the back of this book.

Most people procrastinate handling and solving their inner issues, therefore bigger issues will arise in their Kingdom (inner life). See it like this, you are the reign of your inner Kingdom!

The physical body and psychological functioning are closely related to each other. The mind influences the body, the body influences the mind.

This is **always** the case.

Chinese Traditional Medicine knows 2 types for the human condition.

1. Overfeeding (heart issues, high blood pressure, diabetes)

This means that the body gets things to process that it can't use and/or absorb.

This is an internal problem.

It is like a plant that got too much water, for people it is usually situated in the following areas: too much food, sex, vitamins, alcohol, emotions, thinking, practicing, money, possession, etc.

2. Underfeeding (a lack of water, poor soil type)

The overall physical condition of this type of person is bad.

They have a permanent lack of energy/stamina.

As a first step, you can try to get your energy in order and work on that on a daily basis. This is how you do it:

Go sit down in a spot with enough fresh air, in a chair and in a comfortable position.

Bend your thumbs in the palms of your hands and fold your fingers over it, just like a baby's fist. Place your fists on your hips or over your belly. Enjoy the calmness just like a baby that just has been fed, bathed or diaper changed. Learn how to be like a baby again.

This is what we call 'baby restoration'.

The human body is filled with tensions nowadays, that literally shows itself in the muscles. The goal is to get the body as supple as the body of a newborn baby. This means that we need to let go of all the tensions in our bodies. This is what a big part of the practice focuses on.

What is not natural, and what we literally will not see in nature, is procrastination. Nature itself is spontaneous. All-natural affairs are procrastinated by man in our modern world. We need to restore this ourselves and bring it back to its natural proportions if we want to experience life in good health and wellness.

A baby is not dualistic (divided and distinctive) like we are, it doesn't know the difference between the world and itself.

Balancing emotions through 6 sounds

If the body functions slow down, you will collect air in your body. This causes internal pressure (on the organs) and is created by different vapors. It is important to adjust the inner vapors by paying attention to your breathing, inhaling as well as exhaling.

Chinese Medicine uses 6 sounds to disestablish internal pressure caused by unhealthy stagnant vapors (bodily gasses).

In a well-functioning body, the vapors (bodily gasses) are usually healthy and alimentary.

If you want to cleanse your emotions, there are a couple of ways to do this. The best way is to do this in a natural environment (for example next to a tree). But besides that, the early morning atmosphere is the cleanest before daily life starts and everything (life) comes into motion.

1. Inhale clean air to wash your brain, take a deep breath and hold it for 1 second.

2. Without tension, exhale making one of the sounds and let go of all the negative energy.

The 6 sounds

For every sound, you inhale and exhale 6 times.

1.hsu or Shui (This is whistling with pouted lips, but without the whistling sounds, instead an airflow is created)

- This sound cleanses the upper part of the body, the nervous system, the eyes, and the liver.

2. Six times hoh (The sound of someone who has been crying, with the movement of the belly, making the airflow out sounding like a snore.)

- This sound lets go of your gasses and works on the upper middle part of the body, the chest, heart, and tongue.

- In case of physical weakness, you walk around in circles doing this.

3.fuh or hu (blow out the air between your upper teeth and lower lip, exhaling with little tension)

- This sound benefits the mind, gets rid of heat in the stomach.

4. shih or szzz (Blow out the air through your front teeth while holding your jaws loosely secured)

- This sound benefits the respiratory system

5. whoh (pant or blow like you are blowing out a candle, pout your lips and blow out the air from the lower part of your body)

- This sound benefits the lower parts of your body, perineum, big- and small intestine, and your 'water system' kidneys and bladder.

6. shi (sounds like shhh, like you tell someone to be silent while holding your teeth secured and smiling widely).

- This sound benefits all parts of your body, the lower as well as the middle and upper part.

- This sound gets rid of blockages in the body.

Renewal

Everything follows natural cycles, except maybe if the essence of something transforms in something else. Without recycling the universe would get old. Observation learns that this is not true. At the end of a cycle there is no death or destruction, but renewal.

The closer something stays to its center, the less it will be influenced by cyclic changes. If we do not renew or refresh ourselves, we will get heavy and stagnating.

Every day and every moment that we experience more and are becoming more connected to the outer world, we will get physically and mentally more drained.

Only if we know how to renew ourselves, we can go forward freshly and enthusiastically.

Renewal is cleaning up and elimination of pollution of several sources.

Healing is actually taking care of physical, mental and emotional renewal by disestablishing stagnating energies.

Renewal is more important than holding on to the past.

Renewal is easy, let nature do this for you by spending a lot of time in nature and changing your lifestyle to the natural in every aspect of your life.

If things become big and old, they will transform themselves by becoming small and new again. This is the process of universal evolution.

The mind's role in this process

It is conditioned behavior, we may call it programming, that trained the mind to judge on everything. That's how a form of arrogance has come into creation, which made the mind become ruling about issues that are brought to us by the 'higher Self' (Consciousness).

The mind doesn't accept – That What Is – the flow of life itself.

100

And, it is the mind that causes delay and stagnation.

Why?

Because the mind grabs things, holds on to them, and wishes to translate them or point them out in every possible way. While the 'situation', the life flow, already has passed beyond it.

'Higher Self' is always with you, the mind is just a small part of it and has just a tiny little function in it. The mind can never contain the whole capacity where the 'Higher Self' (Consciousness) exists of, it simply doesn't have the capacity.

Because the mind makes itself appear and pretends to be the Higher Self, large confusion is created and therefore constipation in the life flow is the effect. This may be sensed or felt like blockages or obstructions in the person.

This flow needs to be cleared completely to make sure there aren't any obstructions left. That is why cleaning up our conditioning is the highest priority, so there will be made room for renewal.

Inner (true) nature

The refinement of your own inner energy will eventually lead (return) you to the core of your inner being. This can only be experienced intuitively, there is no way to describe it.

And that is why nobody can explain this to you in an exact expression.

It is only possible to experience it individually, where there can be some sort of deepening, merging into the core of your being with increasing intensity.

This lays untouchable and ungraspable in ourselves, we can only feel this energy as we get more silent and calmer and even get so silent that we become speechless. Then this energy can show itself reluctantly, because it won't be overshadowed with everything-and-nothing, and make its inner presence grow if you make it your priority to remain connected with it.

"It is the Source from where everything may spring. If you try to grasp it, you will lose it."

~ Dao De Jing

Optimist versus Pessimist

The optimist, as well as the pessimist, are appearances within duality. They both fall within the concept of yin and yang.

The optimist is positively loaded.

The pessimist is negatively loaded.

These loads cause fluctuations in energy and therefore create particular experiences.

If you are able to accept that these energies are ruling in this world, see through them, then you can make yourself a Realist.

The Realist sees everything as it is, does not allow himself to be wrapped up by what he sees.

He sees everything as pictures without a load and is therefore neutral. He is involved (manager of situations) and deals with matters. He does not get entangled and sees the 10,000 things for what they are.

Food according to the 5 elements

To bring the body (digestion) back into balance, a deepening knowledge is possible with the nutrition theory according to the 5 elements. There are plenty of tasty and responsible recipes available to make a simple start and adapt your lifestyle to your individual energy type.

Changing your diet also involves listening to your stomach, literally developing a gut feeling, and continuing to develop this for yourself from there by yourself.

If you have digestive problems or energy problems, which may be related to your diet, then you can benefit from a consultation with a nutrition consultant who has been fully introduced in the method of the 5 elements nutritional doctrine.

Get to know the powers of Yin and Yang

Below you find an overview of various opposing forces of Yin and Yang.

The Yin / Yang symbol, the black side (yin) and the white side (yang) represent a continuous movement that infinitely goes on.

The movement is between extremes and in the middle is the middle way in which the practitioner of the teachings of the Dao puts its priority and focus. It is a way of the average, where not too much extremity is experienced and where it is easier to keep balance (in short).

Yin	Yang
Dark	light
Female	Male
Moon	Sun
Rest	Movement
Water	Fire
Empty	Full
Responsive	Creative
Mother	Father
Earth	Heaven
Cold	Heat
Moist	Drought
North	South

How to use the yin-yang symbol

You can simply give the yin/yang symbol a place on everything that moves within the universe. Even on every organ in our body a yin/yang sign can be placed to follow the activity of that organ over the course of a day. But it can also be applied to situations, changes of seasons and phenomena. And if you want to draw the dynamics, you come out on a wavy pattern, similar to the waves in an ocean that rise– shine-dawn continuously.

We advise to study the I Ching and Dao De Jing to gain a broader understanding.

Start with Self-inquiry or self-examination

"If you don't have a plan, you become part of somebody else's plan"
- Unknown author

Why start a self-examination?

You may feel that you have somehow got stuck in your life. This can happen in many areas and is very humanlike and part of life itself. It is not necessary and also not intended to keep you stuck. That is why it may be useful to subject one or another to a further investigation.

Answers that apply to you are not found in the outside world but in yourself.

Unfortunately, we have been taught from childhood that we can find all our answers in the outside world. As a result, our mind has been directed outwards and gone further and further from our infinitely rich inner world. In your inner world, you will find very different answers than you would initially think. These answers are meant solely for you so that you can make your own life journey and get satisfaction from life for yourself.

In each of us, a piece of the puzzle is hidden, but we can also catch glimpses of the Great Whole. Life is actually an adventure, but we have been conditioned to safety and that comes from fear of life itself.

There are indeed no certainties, but we can learn to trust our inner knowing and from there spontaneously take part in life. It is therefore important to be attentive when your inner mood becomes negative, usually, it is an indication that you are not fully connected to the life-current.

The point is that you are going to experience this all by yourself, it yields insights that will let your understanding grow and maybe even surpass it. Life itself is your greatest teacher.

Necessities:

- writing materials (journal and pen)

- a healthy dose of curiosity and desire to discover your inner nature

- the courage to be different than the crowd or flock

-love, care and attention for yourself

How?

You start your own research here and now, from where you are now. Most likely an inner need or questioning arose where you want to get clarity on.

This often has to do with the life experiences that you have gained so far. This is only about you, your experiences in relation to the 'world around you'.

These are all experiences, people, things, situations. It is also often situations that you have experienced or have experienced lately, that raise questions.

For example the question: "What the hell is going on in my life" (or looking at the lives of others in this world)?

Know that these are very normal and healthy life-questions and that your life is meant precisely for this. If this kind of questioning arises in you, it is time to prioritize on answering this call from your inner being. Not everyone in this world has already developed this interest, you will see that it is really your individual search and that it is not always understood by others. Therefore you may need to keep this completely to yourself.

You are going to use your mind (mind and feeling) to take your path back to your earliest memory in this life. You will very consciously follow your own thoughts and hold them back to the light, always asking the question: "Is this true?"

The point is that you put your mind to work to get the truth about yourself unveiled. The mind becomes a kind of detective and will help you to clarify whether the things you think about yourself really represent your inner nature. Or that you are dealing with all kinds of memories stored in an inner database, opinions of others, images, ideas, concepts, assumptions.

We want to tell you in advance that the mind fulfills a double role of itself because it is the mind that unthinkingly engages all those thoughts. And because of that, you are constantly in a state of readiness, stress, and fear, for all kinds of things that you will not even come across. As a result, you have actually become trapped and become your own biggest enemy.

We, therefore, advise you to use your intuition as often as possible so that it can continue to grow and develop. You know, that sometimes pervasive, urgent, inexplicable feeling in yourself that whispers something inside yourself?

Below we already pose a few questions you may start with:

- Am I aware?

- Who is the observer of all things?

- What things in this world are permanent in nature, incorruptible and eternal?

This is a start.

If you use your logbook to take notes of your findings, you can regularly look back at the things you have already done.

Sometimes you can walk around for a while with a certain question without immediately getting an answer. It can even cause a little irritation or another annoying feeling.

111

Know that this is usually temporary, that it is not the intention that you do violence to yourself but lovingly deal with yourself. Usually, you will automatically receive answers to your questions at some point, sometimes even at a moment when you do not even expect it.

But if your curiosity is still not fully answered, then a new question usually comes up, or life itself treats you with a situation where you can 'chew on' for a while. And sometimes life can also treat you with a book in which you find exactly those ingredients that will help you further.

We wish you a lovely journey and a lot of wisdom in Good Chi.

About Chi-Full

Chi-Full is not a Chinese medical practice but works with the Chinese preventive approach in the areas that people can apply for themselves. This includes Chi-Dao Qigong, Zuowang Lun Meditation, consciously dealing with nutrition (according to the 5 elements) and methods to reduce, prevent and release stress.

Chi-full team works from an energetical point of view and can help you to obtain practical insights that make it easier to get along with the rapid changes in this time.

At this moment you work with our basic book, where we explain the broad outlines of our working method. And maybe these are the only things you need for yourself to get your own story solved. They are exactly that group of Universal teachings that are equal for everyone regardless of background, gender, age, etc.

What you do with it for yourself is up to you, maybe the book ends up on the shelf. If you ever pick it up again, you actually pick up where you left off and can move on further by yourself.

Or it does something to you, you feel something starting up in yourself and want to know more about it, then you start your own research and all of a sudden you are on your Way.

We work this way because we know that you have the ability to work through this content step by step. It is about what you think, not what we think or whoever else. All the answers come to you from your own inner thoughts bubbling up and you can feel for yourself what you need at the moment to take another step. Every step you take is processed in a gradual way and gradually becomes integrated.

If you want, we can provide you with more information that is appropriate to the point where you currently are.

You can also participate in workshops and we offer a number of practical exercises that will help you to coordinate your body and mind. You then can continue your practice with what you have learned on a daily basis.

We strive to help you so that your natural inner being can shine as it should be "In Good Chi".

We have more than enough materials, information, and activities to help you out. Chi-Full works from these principles, where the self-healing ability of every person is the center. In order to wake up this ability in you, we have various tools and we offer online modules that will eventually be available on our website.

Chi-Full team has chosen to practice the teachings of the 'Dao of simplicity' and focuses on returning to the individual inner nature (state of being).

114

For those with a wider interest, there are many texts and books to find in which more extensive teaching can be found. However, we have chosen to offer the shortest route. All other stages and knowledge areas are extra tools that can be used based on the personal interest of the student.

Through our website www.chifull.eu we offer online modules on specific topics, which serve as an extension on this basis.

If you have serious or acute medical issues, we always advise to consult a doctor or specialist and to call in the necessary professional medical assistance (disclaimer on our website).

For additional information, E-coaching, E-consultation, workshops and training, books and services, you can contact us by sending an e-mail to

chifull.eu@outlook.com

About the authors

Saskia and Ronald created this book from their own experiences and studies of different teachings from the East and West, bringing it to the rest of the world for educational and inspirational purposes.

There is a profound deepening in our selves, that is what we are pointing at, and you may find it too.

"Let's just keep life simple and natural"

We wish you Good Chi.

Chi-Full Team

We give a big thank you to Esmée for the translation and to our skill-full volunteers for their continuous contribution in our Chi-Full daily life.